AF283979

The Painting in the Attic

By Paul Shipton

Illustrated by Kev Hopgood

Activities by Hannah Fish

Contents

OXFORD
UNIVERSITY PRESS

Ben and Rosie are always ready for a new adventure in Grandpa's amazing van.

The van can fly. It can change shape. It can go anywhere in the world in moments … And it can travel through time!

Ben and Rosie are ready for their next adventure. Are you?

Grandpa Rosie and Ben's grandfather

Clunk Grandpa's robot

Alice and her brother Max Rosie and Ben's friends

Grandma Vera Alice and Max's grandmother

Julia King The owner of an art gallery

Detective Jones A police officer

Imagine!

Rosie and Alice find an old painting in an attic. What happens when the painting is stolen? Read *The Painting in the Attic* to find out!

3

Chapter One

Rosie and Alice were visiting Alice and Max's grandma.
Usually they sat and talked in the kitchen, but today
Grandma Vera asked them to find something in the attic.

The attic was dark and the two girls had to use
flashlights. There were boxes and bags everywhere.
'I don't think that Grandma has been up here in years,'
said Alice.

Rosie was looking behind some books in the corner.
'Hey, look at this,' she said. 'There's an old painting here!'

Rosie picked up the painting and looked at it.
'It's a picture of the countryside,' she said. 'I like it.'
Alice looked at the picture, too. 'Me too! Let's
take it downstairs and ask Grandma Vera about it.'

A few minutes later they
were showing the painting to
Grandma Vera.

'Did you know that this was
in your attic?' asked Rosie.

'No,' said Grandma Vera.
'Perhaps it was already there
when I bought this house.'
She studied the picture. 'It
looks very old.'

→ Go to page 32 for activities.

Grandma Vera began to type at the computer. A minute later, she had the phone number of an art gallery in town.

A woman answered the phone: 'Hello. This is the King Gallery.'

Grandma Vera quickly explained all about the painting from the attic. 'It's a lovely landscape,' she said. 'There are some trees and hills, and there's a little red boat on the sea. The painting's dirty so I can't see any more.'

The woman on the phone sounded interested. 'Give me your address,' she said. 'I'm coming to look at that painting right now!'

Twenty minutes later, a tall woman in expensive clothes was at the door.

'I'm Julia King,' she said. 'I'm here to see the painting.'

Alice took her to the kitchen, where the painting was on the table.

'I'm going to put it in my living room,' said Grandma Vera, 'but I'd like to know more about it first. Can you help?'

'Of course,' Julia said with a smile. 'But I'll have to take it away to my gallery to study it.'

Go to page 33 for activities.

Chapter Two

Grandma Vera didn't hear anything for a few days.

'I'm getting a little worried,' she told Alice and Rosie.

But then they heard the doorbell – Julia King was back. 'I have some news about your painting,' she said.

Grandma Vera was excited. 'Is it very old?'

'No,' said Julia. 'It's just a new copy of an old painting by a famous artist … a *bad* copy. If you tried to sell it, you would get nothing.'

'That's OK,' said Grandma Vera. 'Can I have it back, please?'

'No,' said Julia. 'We were cleaning the painting at the gallery and there was a problem. The cheap, awful paint on it started to come off the canvas. We had to throw it away.'

'But –' Alice started to speak but Julia stopped her. 'The painting was trash. But …' She held out a flat package. 'I can give you another, *nicer* painting as a replacement.'

Grandma looked very surprised. 'Er … thank you.'

→ Go to page 35 for activities.

'You're welcome,' said Julia.

Before Grandma Vera could reply, Julia turned and walked quickly away.

Rosie and Alice watched as she got into her fast, expensive car.

Next to them, Grandma Vera was opening the package that Julia had given her.

'Oh dear,' Grandma Vera said quietly. 'I don't think that I want to put this up in the living room. I don't really like it.'

Rosie and Alice looked at the new painting in Grandma Vera's hands. It was terrible!

That evening at home, Rosie told Grandpa everything that had happened.

'The woman from the art gallery didn't say sorry to Alice's grandma,' she said.

Grandpa asked Rosie to describe the first painting, the one from the attic. He listened carefully, and then he said, 'I can't get the painting back from the art gallery. But I can get Grandma Vera one that's very similar to it.'

'How?' asked Rosie.

Grandpa just smiled and stood up. 'Clunk!' he shouted. 'Where are you?'

→ Go to page 36 for activities.

Chapter Three

Rosie was at home when Alice called her the next day. Alice didn't sound happy on the phone.

'What's wrong?' Rosie asked.

'Can you come to my house?' replied Alice. 'I'll explain everything here. Ask Ben to come too, please. Max is here with me.'

Quickly, Rosie found her brother. Soon they were both at Alice and Max's house.

Alice was waiting for them. 'Come in,' she said. 'You have to see this.'

Julia King

Max was watching the news on TV.

'Listen to this,' he said.

'There's exciting news in the art world,' the newsreader was saying. 'The owner of an art gallery has found a painting by the famous artist Rossi.'

Suddenly Julia King's face was on the TV screen. 'For five hundred years, Rossi has been famous for his landscape paintings,' she said. 'We were very surprised when we found this painting in a room in the basement of my gallery. Surprised and happy, of course.'

→ Go to page 38 for activities.

Then the news showed the painting that Julia was talking about.

'But … this must be a mistake,' said Rosie. 'That's the painting from your grandma's attic. It wasn't found in the gallery's basement!'

Alice picked up her phone. 'I'm going to find out what's happening …' She put the phone to her ear. 'Hello? Is that the King Gallery? I'd like to speak to Ms King, please. It's about the Rossi painting.'

Alice listened for a few seconds and then looked surprised.

'They said that Julia King isn't answering any calls,' said Alice. 'She's too busy.'

'But she's lying about the painting!' said Rosie. 'Why?'

Ben pointed to the TV. The newsreader said, 'The gallery plans to sell the painting next week. Some people think that this might be the most expensive landscape painting *ever*.'

Max turned off the TV. 'That's why,' he said. 'Julia King is going to be very, very rich after she sells the painting.'

Go to page 39 for activities.

Chapter Four

'We have to tell Grandma,' said Max.

'No,' said Alice. 'If we tell her, she'll get worried.'
She turned to Ben and Rosie. 'Can Grandpa help us?'

'We haven't seen Grandpa all day,' said Rosie.
'I don't know where he is.'

Ben stood up. 'We can't wait. Julia King stole that
painting. We have to go and tell the police!'

Twenty minutes later, the four of them were at the
police station. They began to explain everything to
the police officer at the desk.

The police officer wrote in his notebook at first, but then he stopped. 'Are you telling me that you found a famous painting in your grandma's attic?' he asked.

'Yes,' Alice said. 'But we didn't know that it was famous.'

'And then the owner of the King Gallery in town stole this painting?'

'That's right!' said Max.

'And do you have any proof of this?'

The answer was no.

'I'm sorry,' said the police officer. 'We can't do anything without proof.'

→ Go to page 41 for activities.

'What now?' Max asked as they left the station.
'I don't know,' answered Ben.

But then a man ran out of the police station.
'Wait!' he shouted.

The man showed them his police badge.
He didn't wear a uniform but he was a police
officer. 'My name's Detective Jones,' he said.
'I heard you talking to the police officer on
the front desk. I believe your story.'

'Why do *you* believe us?' asked Alice.

Detective Jones pulled out a photo from
his pocket.

'Because for months I've been trying to find proof that this person is a criminal,' he said.

The person in the photo was Julia King.

An hour later, the children and Detective Jones were sitting in the kitchen of Ben and Rosie's house.

'Why can't you just arrest Julia King?' asked Rosie.

'It's not so easy,' said Detective Jones. 'We need proof.'

The door opened and Grandpa walked in. Clunk followed him. In his metal hand the robot held a painting.

A Rossi landscape!

→ Go to page 42 for activities.

Chapter Five

Everyone looked at the painting that Grandpa had brought.

'It's just like the one from Grandma's attic!' Max said.

'How did you make this amazing copy of the painting?' asked Detective Jones.

'There's no time to explain now,' said Grandpa. 'We need a plan.'

Alice was looking at the painting carefully. 'This painting is a little different,' she said. 'And that gives me an idea!'

Alice began to explain and slowly everyone in the room started to smile.

In the morning, Grandpa and the children stood in the crowd outside the art gallery.

Grandma Vera was there, too. She wasn't really sure what was happening. 'Are we here to get my painting back?' she asked.

'I hope so, Grandma,' said Max.

They had to wait for a long time before the doors opened.

As they went inside, Ben asked, 'Where's the painting?'

'Guards are probably watching it in a back room of the gallery,' said Grandpa.

Go to page 44 for activities.

Grandpa was right – the Rossi painting was in a small room, and two guards were with it.

One of them watched the door. The other watched the window. They were ready for anything.

Almost anything.

They didn't hear the noise from above as a hole opened in the ceiling.

They didn't see anything as a robot slowly came down from the ceiling on a rope.

They didn't notice when Clunk took the Rossi painting and put another painting in its place.

A few minutes later, in the biggest room of the gallery, everyone stopped talking as Julia King walked to the front.

She looked around the room and said, 'This is the painting that you have all been waiting for … the Rossi landscape.'

Two guards walked in from a side door and carefully put the painting on an easel.

Julia smiled coldly. 'How much will you pay for this beautiful art?'

Go to page 45 for activities.

Chapter Six

When a gallery sells art like this, nobody knows the price – the painting goes to the person who pays the most money.

One man near the front put his hand in the air.

Then a woman at the back of the room put her hand up.

Then another man.

Every time somebody put up a hand, the painting's price went up. Julia looked happier and happier. She was going to be very, very rich by the end of the day.

But then Julia saw a face in the crowd and she became suddenly angry. She could see the old woman whose attic the painting had come from!

Julia looked again. Those girls were with her, too.

Julia called one of the gallery guards to her. She pointed to Grandma Vera and the two girls.

'Those people are criminals,' she whispered. 'I don't want them in my gallery.'

The guard began to walk across the room.

➔ Go to page 47 for activities.

Suddenly Alice jumped up from her chair and ran to the front of the room.

'Stop!' shouted the guard, but Alice was too fast.

'Get her!' shouted Julia. Two other guards started to run at Alice.

'Wait!' said Alice. 'I have something important to say. Rossi did not really paint this picture!'

'Of course he did!' said Julia. 'Experts have looked at the painting and agreed.'

But Alice pointed at something in the bottom corner of the painting. 'Then what's *this*?' she asked.

A man at the front stood up and moved closer
to the painting. After a few seconds, he looked up.
'It's … a *van*!'

'A van?' said a woman. 'How could a van be in a
painting that's five hundred years old?' She started
to laugh.

Soon more people were laughing.

'Be quiet!' shouted Julia King. 'It isn't funny. This
picture was painted by Rossi!'

But then she, too, saw the van in the painting …

→ Go to page 48 for activities.

Chapter Seven

'This is the wrong painting!' Julia shouted angrily.
'This isn't the painting that I stole from her!' She
pointed at Grandma Vera. 'That picture didn't have
a van in it!'

Suddenly she stopped. Everyone was looking at
her. Had she just said that she *stole* the painting?

A man stood up from
the crowd. 'Excuse me,
Ms King,' said Detective
Jones. 'I think that we
should talk about this
painting. Please come with
me to the police station.'

Later that day, the children went to Grandma Vera's house.

She didn't understand everything that had happened that day. But she was very happy to have the painting from the attic back in her house.

'It's beautiful,' she said.

'If you sell it, you'll get a lot of money, Grandma,' said Max.

'Maybe,' said Grandma Vera. 'But I'd never sell it. I like to look at it.'

'What about the other painting?' asked Rosie. 'The one with the van?'

'*I'm* going to keep that,' said Grandpa.

Go to page 50 for activities.

As they left, Detective Jones turned to Grandpa. 'There's one thing that I don't understand,' said Jones. 'How *did* you get that fantastic copy of the painting?'

Grandpa smiled. 'You'll never believe it,' he said. 'My van can travel in time. I took it hundreds of years into the past and found the famous painter Rossi. I asked him to paint a new landscape and this time to put my van in the painting.'

Jones was laughing. 'You're right,' he said. 'I don't believe it!'

At home, Grandpa went into his room. Clunk followed him. The robot was carrying the painting with the van in it.

'Detective Jones didn't believe me,' Grandpa said. 'He didn't believe that Rossi really painted that picture.'

'Of course not,' answered Clunk. 'But we know that he did.'

He started to put up the painting next to all of Grandpa's other wonderful paintings.

Go to page 51 for activities.

Activities for pages 4–5

1 **Read the sentences. Choose the correct words.**

1 Rosie and Alice _____were_____ visiting Grandma Vera.

   a did   **b** had   ~~**c** were~~

2 Grandma Vera _____ them to find something in the attic.

   a spoke   **b** said   **c** asked

3 In the attic there were boxes and bags _____ .

   a anywhere   **b** everywhere   **c** somewhere

4 Rosie _____ an old painting behind some books.

   a took   **b** found   **c** looked

5 The painting was of the _____ .

   a countryside   **b** country   **c** countrywide

6 They took the painting downstairs to _____ Grandma Vera.

   a show   **b** visit   **c** meet

7 The painting _____ very old.

   a saw   **b** looked   **c** watched

Activities for pages 6–7

1 **Complete the sentences.**

> woman gallery ~~art~~ house painting name

1 Grandma Vera got the number of an _____art_____ gallery.

2 Grandma Vera spoke to a _____ at the King Gallery.

3 The woman was interested in the _____.

4 The woman's _____ was Julia King.

5 Julia King came to Grandma Vera's _____.

6 Julia King took the painting to her _____.

2 **Write *yes* or *no*.**

1 Grandma Vera has a computer.   _____yes_____

2 Grandma Vera used the computer to get a phone number.   _____

3 A woman from the Queen Gallery answered the phone.   _____

4 The painting was a lovely landscape.   _____

5 The painting was dirty.   _____

6 Grandma Vera wanted to put the painting in her kitchen.   _____

7 Grandma Vera wanted to know more about the painting.   _____

8 Julia King couldn't help Grandma Vera.   _____

33

1 **Choose and write the correct words to complete the summary of Chapter One.**

Rosie and Alice were visiting Max and ¹___Alice's___ Grandma. The girls went ²_____ to the attic to find something ³_____ Grandma Vera. The attic was ⁴_____. Rosie found an old painting ⁵_____ some books. The painting was a landscape with ⁶_____ trees and hills and a little boat ⁷_____ the sea. Julia King ⁸_____ the King Gallery came to see the painting. She said that she could ⁹_____ Grandma Vera, but she wanted ¹⁰_____ the painting to her gallery.

1 its   her   ~~Alice's~~

2 on   up   at

3 to   from   for

4 dark   darker   darkly

5 between   behind   before

6 them   more   some

7 at   on   to

8 from   where   that

9 helping   help   helped

10 take   could take   to take

Talk **Are there any paintings in your house? Talk to a friend.**

1 Choose and write the correct words.

> a gallery   ~~trash~~   a doorbell
> famous   canvas   an artist

1 This is something that is no longer
needed or useful. We throw it away. _____trash_____

2 We use this word to describe a person
that everybody knows. _____

3 We use this to tell someone that we are at
their door. It makes a noise inside the house. _____

4 This person paints pictures. _____

5 This is a place that shows paintings
and other art. _____

6 Artists often paint pictures on this. _____

2 Circle the mistakes. Then write the correct words.

1 Grandma Vera didn't hear anything
for a (little) days. _____few_____

2 But then Julia King were back. _____

3 Julia had some news for the painting. _____

4 Julia said Grandma Vera's painting
was a badly copy. _____

5 Julia told the painting was trash. _____

6 But Grandma Vera wanting the painting back. _____

7 Julia gave Grandma Vera some replacement. _____

8 Grandma Vera was very surprising. _____

Activities for pages 10–11

1 Choose the correct answers.

1 Julia King got into her …

    a small, cheap car.　**b** old, damaged car.
    c fast, expensive car.

2 In the package there was …

    a a beautiful painting.　**b** a terrible painting.
    c a good painting.

3 Grandpa said that he could get …

    a a similar painting.　**b** the painting back.
    c a better painting.

2 Look at the picture on page 11 and write *yes* or *no*.

1 Grandpa and Rosie are in the kitchen.　_yes_

2 Grandpa is talking to Rosie.　_____

3 Rosie is sitting down.　_____

4 Rosie is wearing blue jeans and a red sweater.　_____

5 Grandpa is wearing a black jacket and
   blue pants.　_____

6 On the table there are two cups.　_____

7 Behind Grandpa there is a painting on the wall.　_____

8 Behind Rosie there is an open window.　_____

1 Circle the correct words.

1 Grandma Vera (didn't) / **did** hear anything for a few days.

2 But then they heard the **phone** / **doorbell**.

3 Julia King had **something** / **some news** about Grandma Vera's painting.

4 She said that it was a **copier** / **copy** of an old painting.

5 Julia said that they had **thrown** / **put** the painting away.

6 She **gave** / **sold** Grandma Vera a replacement.

7 Grandma Vera didn't **like** / **liked** the replacement.

8 Rosie told **Grandpa** / **Grandma** everything that had happened.

2 Order the events in Chapter Two.

Julia gave Grandma Vera a package.   _____

Julia said that Grandma Vera's painting was a bad copy. _____

Rosie told Grandpa everything that had happened.   _____

Julia King came to Grandma Vera's house.   __1__

Julia said that they had thrown Grandma Vera's
painting away.   _____

Grandpa said that he could get a similar painting
to Grandma Vera's.   _____

Talk **Do you think Julia threw Grandma Vera's painting away?
Tell a friend your ideas.**

1 Choose the correct answers.

1 Alice asked Rosie …

  a to find the painting.   **b** to go to the gallery.
  c to come to her house.

2 Alice was waiting for …

  a Rosie and Grandpa.   **b** Rosie and Ben.
  c Ben and Grandpa.

3 Max was watching …

  a a computer game.   **b** the news on TV.
  c an art gallery on TV.

4 There was exciting news in …

  a the animal world.   **b** the police world.
  c the art world.

5 Suddenly Julia King was …

  a on the TV screen.   **b** at the door.
  c talking to Grandma.

6 Julia King said that they had …

  a bought a painting.   **b** seen a painting.
  c found a painting.

1 **Look at pages 14 and 15 and complete the sentences. You can use 1, 2, 3, or 4 words.**

1 Then the news _showed the painting_ that Julia was talking about.

2 It was the painting _____ attic.

3 Alice called the _____ Gallery.

4 Alice asked _____ King.

5 Julia King wasn't _____ calls.

6 The gallery was planning _____ painting.

7 It might be the _____ landscape painting ever.

2 **Match. Then write what the children say.**

1 'That's the painting • • the painting! Why?'

2 'It wasn't found in • • the painting next week.'

3 'But she's lying about • • from your grandma's attic.'

4 'The gallery plans to sell • • the gallery's basement!'

1 _'That's the painting from your grandma's attic.'_

2 _____

3 _____

4 _____

Activities to review Chapter Three (pages 12–15)

1 **Choose the correct answers.**

1 Alice didn't sound happy when she called Rosie.

a Right **b** Wrong **c** Doesn't say

2 Alice had been crying before she called Rosie.

a Right **b** Wrong **c** Doesn't say

3 Max was watching the news on his computer.

a Right **b** Wrong **c** Doesn't say

4 The news said that the King Gallery had found a painting.

a Right **b** Wrong **c** Doesn't say

5 They said that the painting was by the famous artist Rossi.

a Right **b** Wrong **c** Doesn't say

6 Alice went to the King Gallery to talk to Julia.

a Right **b** Wrong **c** Doesn't say

7 Julia King didn't want the children to find out about the painting.

a Right **b** Wrong **c** Doesn't say

8 The gallery was planning to sell the painting.

a Right **b** Wrong **c** Doesn't say

Talk **What do the children do?**
Tell a friend your ideas.

1 **Order the words.**

1 went to / the / children / police / The / station.

   The children went to the police station.

2 explained / to / police officer. / They / everything / the

   _____

3 in / The / notebook. / police / wrote / officer / his

   _____

4 asked / some / the children / The / questions. /
   police officer

   _____

5 didn't / any / the / proof. / But / have / children

   _____

2 **Who said this? Write the names.**

1 'We have to go and tell the police!'   *Ben*

2 'We can't do anything without proof.'   _____

3 'Can Grandpa help us?'   _____

4 'But we didn't know that it was famous.'   _____

5 'If we tell her, she'll get worried.'   _____

6 'And then the owner of the King Gallery
   in town stole this painting?'   _____

7 'We haven't seen Grandpa all day.'   _____

8 'We have to tell Grandma.'   _____

1 **Find and write the words.**

1 These are special clothes people
wear at work. u _n_ _i_ _f_ _o_ _r_ _m_

2 This is when you think something is true. b _ _ _ _ _ _ _

3 This person does something that
is against the law. c _ _ _ _ _ _ _ _

4 This is when a police officer takes a
criminal to the police station. a _ _ _ _ _ _

5 This is a hard material. Cars are made of this. m _ _ _ _ _

6 This is a type of police officer. d _ _ _ _ _ _ _ _ _

2 **Choose the correct answers to complete
the conversations.**

1 So she stole your grandma's painting?

a Thank you! **b** Oh no! **c** That's right!

2 When did this happen?

a In two weeks. **b** Since two weeks. **c** Two weeks ago.

3 How did she get the painting?

a She's at Grandma Vera's house.
b She came to Grandma Vera's house.
c Grandma Vera went to the gallery.

4 Where is the painting now?

a At her gallery. **b** To her gallery. **c** For her gallery.

1 **Choose and write the correct words to complete the summary of Chapter Four.**

The children ¹ _decided_ to tell the police about Julia King. They went to the police station and ² _____ the police officer everything. But the police officer said that he couldn't do anything without ³ _____. As they were ⁴ _____ the police station, a man ran after them. His name was Detective Jones. He showed them a ⁵ _____. The photo was of Julia King. Detective Jones wanted to find proof that Julia King was a ⁶ _____.

> told police station ran leaving photo
> proof ~~decided~~ thought criminal

Now tick (✓) the best name for Chapter Four.

Going to the gallery ☐

Going to find Grandpa ☐

Going to the police ☐

Talk **How did Grandpa and Clunk get a Rossi landscape? Tell a friend your ideas.**

Activities for pages 20–21

1 **Complete the sentences.**

> idea   copy   hoping   morning   doors   different

1 Grandpa had a _____ of Grandma Vera's painting.

2 The copy was a little _____ to Grandma Vera's painting.

3 That gave Alice an _____.

4 In the _____, they all went to the art gallery.

5 They were _____ to get Grandma Vera's painting back.

6 They waited for a long time before the _____ opened.

2 **Write *yes* or *no*.**

1 Grandpa had brought a painting.   _____

2 Grandpa's painting was the same as Grandma Vera's.   _____

3 Alice told everyone about her idea.   _____

4 There was a crowd outside the art gallery.   _____

5 Grandma Vera didn't want her painting back. _____

6 Ben could see the painting inside the gallery. _____

7 They didn't wait long to go into the gallery. _____

8 Guards were probably watching the painting. _____

1 **Read the sentences. Choose the correct words.**

1 The Rossi painting was in a _____ room with two guards.

    a young **b** short **c** small

2 The guards were ready for _____ anything.

    a almost **b** some **c** most

3 Clunk _____ down from the ceiling on a rope.

    a saw **b** came **c** was

4 Clunk took the Rossi painting and put _____ in its place.

    a new one **b** a different **c** another

5 Julia King walked to the _____ of the room.

    a face **b** front **c** top

6 The guards _____ put the painting on an easel.

    a careful **b** carefully **c** caring

Talk **What do you think happens next?**
What is Alice's idea?
Tell a friend your ideas.

1 Answer the questions.

1 What was Grandpa's painting like?

   It was just like the one from Grandma Vera's attic.

2 Why did they all go to the art gallery?

   _____

3 Where was the Rossi painting?

   _____

4 What did Clunk do?

   _____

5 Why did Julia King smile coldly?

   _____

2 Order the events in Chapter Five.

Clunk opened a hole in the ceiling.   _____

Alice looked at Grandpa's painting carefully.   _____

Julia King walked to the front of the room.   _____

Grandpa brought a copy of Grandma Vera's painting.   _____

Clunk took the Rossi painting.   _____

Alice had an idea.   _____

The guards put the painting on an easel.   _____

They all went into the art gallery.   _____

1 **Choose and write the correct words.**

Nobody knew the ¹_____ of the painting.
The painting would go to the person ²_____ paid the
most money. Every time ³_____ put up their
⁴_____, the price got higher. Julia King looked
happier and ⁵_____. But then she saw a face
⁶_____ the crowd. She became ⁷_____. Julia
saw Alice, Rosie, and Grandma Vera. Julia called to
⁸_____ the gallery guards. She pointed ⁹_____
the girls and Grandma Vera. The guard began to walk over
to ¹⁰_____.

1 money price pay	**6** in at on
2 who what where	**7** anger angrilly angry
3 nobody somebody everybody	**8** one's one of one
4 money painting hand	**9** with to from
5 happiest happy happier	**10** theirs they them

Talk **What will the guard do? Talk to a friend.**

47

🌀 **Activities** for pages 26–27

1 Choose the correct answers.

1 Alice ran to the back of the room.

    a Right   **b** Wrong   **c** Doesn't say

2 Julia wanted the guards to get Alice.

    a Right   **b** Wrong   **c** Doesn't say

3 When Alice saw the guards, she was afraid.

    a Right   **b** Wrong   **c** Doesn't say

4 Alice said that Rossi did not paint the picture.

    a Right   **b** Wrong   **c** Doesn't say

5 Alice pointed at something on the back of the painting.

    a Right   **b** Wrong   **c** Doesn't say

6 Lots of people in the crowd were looking at Alice.

    a Right   **b** Wrong   **c** Doesn't say

7 There was a picture of a van in the painting.

    a Right   **b** Wrong   **c** Doesn't say

8 Some people in the crowd started laughing.

    a Right   **b** Wrong   **c** Doesn't say

1 **Write the words from Chapter Six.**

1 r c i e p _____price_____

2 x r e p e t _____

3 u y n f n _____

4 r n i m c i l a _____

5 a d r u g _____

6 r e d n h u d _____

7 w r d o c _____

8 n e m o y _____

2 **Match. Then write the sentences.**

up from her chair.

1 Julia thought that •

2 But then she saw •

3 Julia told a guard to •

4 But Alice jumped •

get them out of the gallery.

she was going to be rich.

Alice, Rosie, and Grandma Vera.

1 _____

2 _____

3 _____

4 _____

1 **Order the words.**

1 that / had / Julia / the / painting. / said / stolen / she

_____

2 took / the / Detective Jones / police station. / to / Julia

_____

3 to have / happy / back. / Grandma Vera / was / painting / her

_____

4 Grandma Vera / at / painting. / liked / to look / the

_____

5 the van. / Grandpa / the / kept / with / painting

_____

2 **Look at the picture on page 29 and write *yes* or *no*.**

1 There are eight people in the room.   _____

2 Rosie is sitting down and has a drink.   _____

3 Grandpa is drinking a cup of tea.   _____

4 Ben and Max are holding up a painting.   _____

5 In the painting there is a red boat on a lake.   _____

6 Grandma Vera is wearing glasses.   _____

7 There are some beautiful flowers behind
Grandma Vera.   _____

8 Ben has one hand in his pocket.   _____

❀ Activities for pages 30–31

1 Circle the correct words.

1 Grandpa **had** / **was** traveled into the past.

2 Grandpa found **a** / **the** famous painter Rossi.

3 Rossi painted a **new** / **newly** landscape for Grandpa.

4 Rossi put Grandpa's van in **he's** / **his** new painting.

5 Detective Jones didn't **believe** / **believing** Grandpa.

6 Clunk **put** / **got** up the painting in Grandpa's room.

2 Choose the correct answers to complete the conversations.

1 How did you get the painting?

  a I wanted the van.   **b** I got a van.   **c** I used my van.

2 Where did you go?

  a back in time   **b** before in time   **c** then in time

3 Who did you talk to?

  a the painter Rossi   **b** a painter Rossi
  c that painter Rossi

4 Did he paint a new landscape?

  a Why not?   **b** Yes, he did.   **c** Yes, please.

5 What was in the new landscape?

  a My van!   **b** Mine van!   **c** His van!

1 Choose and write the correct words to complete the summary of Chapter Seven.

Julia was very ¹_____. She shouted and pointed at Grandma Vera. Suddenly everyone looked at her. She said that she had ²_____ the painting from Grandma Vera! Detective Jones stood up and said, 'Please come with me to the police station.' Grandma Vera was very ³_____ to have her painting back. Detective Jones asked Grandpa about the painting with the ⁴_____. Grandpa told him how he had got it, but Detective Jones didn't ⁵_____ him. Clunk followed Grandpa to his ⁶_____. He put up the new painting next to all of Grandpa's other wonderful paintings.

> police station   angry   painting   van
> believe   room   stolen   told   happy   afraid

Now tick (✓) the best name for Chapter Seven.

Rossi's painting is beautiful ☐

Rossi's painting is a copy ☐

Rossi's painting is home ☐

Talk Do you like this story? Talk to a friend.

Art Research

1 **Do some Internet research. Choose a painting you like. Find out about the painting and answer the questions.**

What is the name of the painting? _____

_____

Who is the artist? _____

_____

Where is the artist from? _____

_____

Is the artist famous? _____

_____

When did the artist paint the picture? _____

_____

What can you see in the painting? _____

_____

_____

What is special about the painting? _____

_____

_____

2 **Display some information about the painting you chose. Write the answers to the questions above, and add a picture of the painting.**

Glossary

Here are some words used in this book, and you can check what they mean. Use a dictionary to check other new words.

arrest *verb*
When the police arrest someone, they take that person away to ask them questions about a crime.

art gallery *noun*
a place where people can look at or buy art

artist *noun*
a person who makes art

attic *noun*
the space under the roof of a house

badge *noun*
a piece of metal, cloth, or plastic with a design or words on it that you wear on your clothes

basement *noun*
a room or space in a building that is under the ground

believe *verb*
to feel sure that something is true

canvas *noun*
a strong heavy cloth, used to paint pictures on

clean *verb*
to remove the dirt or marks from something

cold *adjective*
not friendly or kind

copy *noun*
a thing that is made to look exactly like another thing

countryside *noun*
land with fields, woods, farms, etc. that is away from towns and cities

criminal *noun*
a person who does something that is against the law

dark *adjective*
with no light, or not much light

detective *noun*
a person whose job is to find out who did a crime

dirty *adjective*
not clean

easel *noun*
a frame that an artist uses to hold a picture while it is being painted

exciting *adjective*
not calm, for example because you are happy about something that is going to happen

explain *verb*
to tell someone about something so that they understand it

flat *adjective*
smooth, with no parts that are higher or lower than the rest

guard *noun*
a person who keeps something safe from other people

landscape *noun*
everything you can see in an area of land

lie *verb*
to say something that you know is not true

mistake *noun*
something that you think or do that is wrong

news *noun*
information about things that have just happened

newsreader *noun*
a person who reads the news on TV or radio

owner *noun*
a person who has something that belongs to them

package *noun*
something that is in a box or bag, or is wrapped in paper

painting *noun*
a picture that someone makes with paint

price *noun/adjective/verb*
how much money you have to pay for something

proof *noun*
information that shows that something is true

replacement *noun*
a new or different thing that takes the place of another

similar *adjective*
the same in some ways but not completely the same

steal *verb*
to secretly take something that is not yours

throw something away *verb*
to get rid of something you don't want

trash *noun*
garbage; things you do not want anymore

whisper *verb*
to speak very quietly to someone, so that people cannot hear what you are saying

worried *adjective*
unhappy because you think that something bad will happen, or that something bad has happened

Definitions in this glossary are taken and adapted from Oxford American Dictionaries for learners of English

Oxford Read and Imagine

Oxford Read and Imagine graded readers are at nine levels (Early Starter, Starter, Beginner, and Levels 1 to 6) for students from age 3 or 4 and older. They offer great stories to read and enjoy.

Activities provide Cambridge Young Learners Exams preparation. See Key below.

At Levels 1 to 6, every storybook reader links to an **Oxford Read and Discover** non-fiction reader, giving students a chance to find out more about the world around them, and an opportunity for Content and Language Integrated Learning (CLIL).

For more information about **Read and Imagine**, and for Teacher's Notes, go to
www.oup.com/elt/teacher/readandimagine

KEY

 F Activity supports Cambridge Young Learners Flyers Exam preparation

KET Activity supports Cambridge Key English Test Exam preparation

 Oxford Read and Discover

Do you want to find out more about art? To find out about landscapes and cities in art from around the world, you can read this non-fiction book.

Our World In Art

OXFORD
UNIVERSITY PRESS

Great Clarendon Street, Oxford, OX2 6DP, United Kingdom

Oxford University Press is a department of the University of Oxford. It furthers the University's objective of excellence in research, scholarship, and education by publishing worldwide. Oxford is a registered trade mark of Oxford University Press in the UK and in certain other countries

ISBN: 978 0 19 473720 3

Printed in China

This book is printed on paper from certified and well-managed sources

ACKNOWLEDGEMENTS

Main illustrations by: Kev Hopgood/Beehive Illustration.